TEAM RESCUE

Sophie McKenzie

Illustrated by **Marina Pérez Luque**

OXFORD
UNIVERSITY PRESS

Letter from the Author

This story is about an ordinary boy called Frank and how he gets involved in an exciting seaside rescue attempt!

The story was inspired by holidays in England that I used to go on when I was a child – and how much fun it is to explore the beach, even when the weather is so windy you can't hear each other speak!

It's also about how initial impressions can be deceptive and that most of the time it's good to get to know people a bit before deciding whether we like them or not. It's also about accepting help from our friends when we're afraid. We don't have to face up to our fears all alone.

I hope you enjoy going on Frank's adventure with him!

Sophie McKenzie

Chapter 1
Looking for Shells

Frank ran as hard as he could. It was a sunny day, but the wind whipped at his face as he raced along the beach. He glanced sideways. *Oh, no.* His cousin Lara was already a stride ahead of him. Frank pushed himself harder. Faster.

His breath burned in his lungs as he tried to catch Lara. The picnic rug was just a few metres away. Another few seconds and …

No. Lara reached the picnic rug first. She threw her hands in the air and let out a happy whoop. Annoyed, Frank flopped onto the rug. His mum ruffled his hair.

'Never mind, Frankie.' She gave him a sympathetic smile, then turned to Frank's little sister Betty, and pulled a face at her. Betty gurgled up at Mum.

Frank frowned. Mum didn't understand. It wasn't fair that Lara beat him. She had longer legs and was almost a whole year older than he was.

'Well done, Lara.' Uncle Pete winked at his daughter.

Lara grinned and danced around the rug. 'I won, I won, I won!' she chanted.

Frank slumped down, poking at the fringing on the picnic rug. He'd been really looking forward to this trip to the seaside, but so far it had been a complete disaster. The bay where they were sitting was a big, empty beach surrounded by high rocks in a semicircle that reached down to the sea. It was very windy, but he didn't mind that. No, the problem was that nobody else was here. The beach was deserted.

Frank pushed the edge of the picnic rug into the sand. If only some of his friends from school were with him. Instead, he was stuck with his aunt and uncle – plus Lara, of course – as well as Mum's friend, Sally, and her teenage daughter, Amy, and new stepson, Kai.

6

Kai was about the same age as Lara and Frank, and all the grown-ups kept saying how great it was that the three of them could play together. Frank couldn't see anything great about it at all. Lara was super annoying, while Kai had barely said a word since they arrived; he had just shaken his head when Lara suggested the race along the sand earlier.

'Time for a new activity!' Uncle Pete clapped his hands together. 'I want you three kids to collect some shells.' He picked up a large red bucket from the edge of the rug and handed it to Lara. 'Fun, eh?'

Lara nodded. 'I love collecting shells,' she said.

Frank sighed. Kai said nothing.

'I fancy a cup of tea,' Mum said.

'Ooh, yes,' Uncle Pete agreed.

'And maybe an ice cream?' Sally suggested.

'Yes, please,' Lara, Frank and Amy said at the same time.

Kai nodded.

'OK,' Uncle Pete clapped his hands together. 'Here's the plan. Us grown-ups will take Betty and head to the ice-cream stand over the rocks – it's not far away. Amy will stay here and keep an eye on the rest of you.'

'I don't need keeping an eye on,' Lara said, crossly.

That's the first sensible thing she's said all day, Frank thought.

'Are you OK with that, Amy?' Sally asked. 'We'll only be gone ten minutes or so.'

Amy glanced up from her phone. 'Sure,' she said.

Mum frowned as she turned to Frank. 'You're not allowed to leave this bay. Or climb on the rocks.'

'And no splashing about in the sea, either,' added Sally.

'You hear that, Frank?' Mum asked.

'Of course, Mum,' Frank replied, rolling his eyes. He glanced at Kai, who gave him a shy smile in return.

'We'll be back before you know it.' Uncle Pete jumped to his feet. 'Now remember, the idea is to include *every* type of shell, big and small, patterned and plain ... to leave no shell unturned!' Uncle Pete laughed. So did the other adults.

Frank sighed again.

A few minutes later the grown-ups, plus Betty, had trundled off across the sand.

'Come on, then,' Lara ordered. 'You two can bring me the shells you find, and I'll decide whether to put them in the bucket.'

'OK,' said Kai.

'That's not fair,' grumbled Frank.

'Yes, it is,' Lara insisted, standing up. 'It was *my* Dad's idea to collect the shells.'

Frank stood up, too. He glared at her. Lara, with her unfairly long legs, was just *too* irritating for words.

'Yeah, Frank,' Amy drawled. 'You need to do what Lara said. Just make sure you stay on the beach.' She tugged a pair of headphones over her ears and settled back on the rug.

'I'm *not* picking up shells,' Frank hissed at Lara.

Lara opened her mouth to speak again, but Kai got there first.

'I'll look with you, Lara,' he said softly. 'I've never collected shells before.'

'Oh, great,' muttered Frank. He grabbed his football. 'I'm going to play with this. See ya!'

'Come back, Frank!' Lara ordered.

Frank ignored her. He kicked his ball along the beach and ran after it. There was no way he was joining in with anything as boring as shell collecting. And certainly not with those two!

Chapter 2
The End of the Beach

Frank kicked the ball towards the sea. It stopped a few metres from the water, where the sand was damp and firm. The waves surged, sucking at the pebbles and shells that were scattered across the beach.

'Frank!' Lara called.

Reluctantly, Frank turned to face her. Lara had followed him down to the shore. She frowned at him, her hands on her hips. The wind from the sea was strong, and her long plaits rippled out behind her. Kai had crouched down beside her. He was exploring the sand for shells with the large red bucket beside him.

Frank braced himself, expecting Lara to demand that he got to work straightaway, but instead, Lara smiled.

'Kick it to me, then,' she said, pointing to the ball.

Frank stared at her, suspiciously. Was she actually agreeing to play with him? Or was this a trick? If he kicked the ball to her, would she run off with it? Or would she – even worse – just pick it up and throw it into the sea?

'No,' he replied. He turned and kicked the ball as hard as he could along the damp sand. Without looking back, he sprinted off after it, towards the rocks at the tip of the bay. The tang of salty sea air filled his nostrils as he raced after the ball, kicking it then racing after it again.

After a minute, he stopped and flopped onto the sand, out of breath. A seagull screeched overhead.

'Frank!' Lara shouted.

He looked up as she jogged over, Kai at her side.

'That was mean, you not kicking me the ball,' Lara snapped, standing over him. 'I thought maybe we could play football *as well* as look for shells.'

Frank stared at her, feeling awkward. He didn't know what to say.

Kai held up a large, delicate pink shell. He turned it towards the sun so that it gleamed, almost transparent in the light.

Frank gazed at the shell, transfixed.

'Isn't it beautiful?' Kai breathed, his dark eyes wide with excitement. 'I've never seen anything so perfect.'

It was lovely, Frank had to admit, but that didn't make collecting shells any less dull.

'It's gorgeous, Kai. Well done,' Lara said. 'It's our best one so far.'

Kai laid his shell carefully in the bucket. 'D'you want to help now, Frank?' he asked quietly.

'I told you – I'm just going to play football,' Frank muttered.

'That's not fair, Frank.' Lara frowned. 'You're leaving me and Kai to do all the work.'

Frank shrugged, then jumped to his feet and sped off again.

The wind roared in his ears as he zigzagged along the shore. It was a sunny day, but out here where the beach was so open the tips of his nose and ears stung with cold. He kicked the ball hard, and it disappeared behind a big clump of seaweed on the sand at the end of the bay.

As Frank ran to find it, a strange sound stopped him in his tracks. It was the sound of something whimpering.

Chapter 3
A Gap in the Rocks

Frank stared at the stretch of high rocks in front of him. He was at the tip of the curve of the bay. On his left was the main part of the beach and to his right, just a few metres away, was the open sea. His football lay on the beach beside him, but he barely noticed it. He was listening out for the whimpering sound.

A moment later, it echoed towards him again.

Where was it coming from? Frank glanced all around. No one was in sight. He looked back the way he had come across the beach, to where Lara and Kai were busily picking up shells. Beyond them, further up on the sand, Amy was just visible, still lying on the picnic rug.

There was no sign of any of the grown-ups.

The whimpering cry sounded a third time. Frank frowned. Was it coming from *inside* the rocks?

26

Frank crept closer to the rock face. A crack ran all the way from the ground to a point just above his head. Was that an opening?

He peered past the crack into the dark space beyond. Excitement pulsed through him.

This was a cave.

Frank turned sideways, drawing in his breath. There was barely enough room for him to squeeze inside. He eased himself into the cave. The hairs on the back of his neck rose as the darkness enveloped him.

'Hello?' he said. 'Who's there?'

Another low whimper. Then a scratching sound.

Frank blinked, letting his eyes adjust to the dim light. He was in a small, hollow space with just enough room for him to stand up. A caramel-coloured dog was curled up on the damp sand on the cave floor. One front paw clawed at the ground. The dog gazed up at Frank, her big, sad eyes gleaming in the sliver of light from the beach outside.

Frank stared at the animal. Fear churned in his stomach. It was obvious the dog was hurt in some way, and Frank wanted to help, but he had always been scared of dogs. He didn't like the way they barked and leaped up at you.

'Frank? Are you in here?' Lara's voice echoed faintly towards him. A second later, she squeezed inside the cave, closely followed by Kai. For the first time all day, Frank was pleased to see them.

Lara's eyes widened as she saw the dog. 'What's she doing in here?'

'I think she's hurt,' Frank said.

'Oh, you poor thing.' Kai eased his way past the others and crouched down carefully next to the dog. He gently stroked her head and rubbed her floppy ears.

Frank watched him in amazement. After hardly speaking all morning, Kai had suddenly lost all his shyness.

'Look.' Kai held up a tangle of old fishing net, plastic straws and food wrapping. 'She's got her paw tangled up in all this rubbish.' Kai gave the net a gentle tug. The dog let out another whimper, which sounded sharper this time.

Frank stepped back quickly, his heart thudding. Was the dog getting angry?

But Kai didn't seem scared at all. He kept trying to untangle the dog's paw, but her whining just grew louder. 'I can't get her free,' he said helplessly. He let go of the mess of rubbish and stroked the dog's back.

The dog sniffed at Kai's hand, settling back onto the sand as he patted her fur.

'This isn't good,' Lara said in a worried voice.

'I know,' Frank murmured. 'Mum says trapped or hurt animals can get so scared they lash out, and this dog might—'

'It's not that.' Lara pointed to the cave's entrance. 'The tide's coming in!'

33

Frank hurried to the crack in the rock face and squeezed out onto the beach. To his horror, he realized that while they'd been in the cave, the sea had crept closer and closer. There was hardly any sand visible, and the waves were almost lapping at his toes.

Lara joined him outside. 'The tide's coming in fast,' she said. 'Which means— '

Frank met her gaze. ' ... which means we need to get that dog out of the cave before it fills with water.'

Chapter 4
Rising Tide

Frank and Lara stood on the beach just outside the cave. The wind roared in their ears as they looked at each other.

'We need scissors or ... or something to cut the dog free,' Frank said.

Lara nodded. She waved her arms at Amy, who was moving their things up the beach, away from the incoming tide.

'Amy!' she yelled. 'We need something sharp!'

But Amy just waved back, clearly oblivious to what Lara was saying.

'It's no good.' Frank's mouth felt dry, panic rising inside him. The waves were almost at their feet. 'Amy can't hear you over the wind.'

Lara stared at him, the horror in her eyes reflecting how he felt. 'But we have to get the dog out!'

'I'll run back to Amy and find something to cut the dog free,' Frank said. 'If I can't see anything, I'll try and find the grown-ups. They must be on their way back from the ice-cream stand by now.'

'No, I'll go,' Lara said. 'I'm faster than you.'

Frank gritted his teeth. Lara was right, though he didn't want to admit it. Part of him wanted to argue with her, to insist that he'd found the dog, so he should be the one to go for help. But he knew in his heart that helping a hurt animal was more important than winning any race. Or any argument.

'OK,' he said. 'Go!'

Lara sped off across the beach.

Frank hurried back to the cave.

Kai was still crouched down next to the dog, whose head was now resting on his knee. He looked up as Frank squeezed through the narrow entrance.

'I've been looking at the way her paw is caught up, and I think I can get her free,' Kai said. 'I need you to hold her still while I do it. OK?'

Frank blinked in surprise. It was as if Kai had turned into a different person. He seemed so much more sure of himself than when they'd met earlier.

Frank, on the other hand, felt about as unsure as he'd ever done in his life.

'Hold the dog?' he asked warily. His throat felt dry.

Kai tilted his head to one side. 'She won't hurt you, Frank,' he said.

Frank fidgeted from foot to foot, his insides churning. 'Maybe ... er, maybe we don't need to free her ourselves,' he stammered. 'Lara's gone to get something to cut the net. She'll be back any moment.'

As he spoke, a wave dribbled into the cave and hissed across the sand.

'We can't wait,' Kai insisted. 'Please, Frank. The dog needs our help.'

'I know she does,' Frank snapped.
He turned away, unable to bear the insistent look in Kai's eyes.

A few long seconds passed.

'Are you ... *scared*?' Kai sounded incredulous.

Frank turned slowly back round to face him. Their eyes met, just as another wave trickled into the cave.

Frank gave a slow, miserable nod. 'Yes,' he said.

Chapter 5
Team Rescue

Kai bent over the dog, rubbing the top of her head gently.

'Hey, it's OK,' he said in a soothing voice.

He was looking at the dog, but Frank had the strong impression Kai was really talking to him.

'It's going to be all right,' Kai went on.

Frank gritted his teeth. It wasn't going to be all right! The sea was coming in too fast. The poor dog was going to be trapped in here if he didn't help Kai free her.

The thought made him tremble with fear. He hurried to the cave entrance and peered out. The waves were lapping at the rocks outside. Across the beach he could see Lara. She and Amy were frantically picking up all the bags on the picnic rug and tipping their contents out. They must still be looking for something they could use to cut the dog free.

Frank's stomach plummeted to his feet. They weren't going to find anything. Nobody takes sharp scissors to a picnic!

It was up to him and Kai.

He went over to the dog and peered down. She gazed up at him, her big, dark eyes sad. Kai looked up at him, too.

'Stroke her fur,' Kai said softly. 'Go on. She's really friendly.'

Frank took a deep breath and reached out his hand. His fingers trembled as he touched the top of the dog's head. Her fur was soft and fine.

'Go on,' Kai urged again. 'A bit firmer, so she can properly feel you.'

Frank pressed his hand against the dog's head, then ran it down her neck. Her fur felt warm under his fingers. He ran his hand back up the dog's neck.

'No, don't ruffle up her fur,' Kai instructed. 'My dog hates that. You should always go in one direction – *down* the fur.'

'OK,' Frank said. He stroked the dog again. She turned her head, nuzzling into his palm. Her nose was surprisingly damp and cold.

'Hey, she likes you.' Frank could hear Kai was smiling, but he kept his eyes on the dog.

'I like *her*,' he said, realizing with surprise that he actually meant it.

'Yeah, she's lovely.' Kai turned to the netting tangled around her paw. 'Just keep stroking her for me. Now I've got two hands free, I think I can get this loose.'

Frank kept stroking the dog, while Kai worked patiently at loosening the net.

A loud splash of water against rock made both boys turn their heads towards the cave entrance. Another wave was already smacking at the rock, then sucking itself away. They looked at each other anxiously.

At this rate, the cave would fill with water in minutes.

'Hurry,' Frank said.

'There!' Kai held up the mess of tangled fishing net he'd untied. His eyes gleamed with triumph. 'She's free. Off you go, girl.'

The dog let out a bark, then rose to her feet. She scampered across the cave as Frank and Kai watched, then disappeared through the opening.

'Brilliant! She's not even injured,' Kai said, with relief.

'Come on, let's go,' Frank said, as another wave splashed at the cave entrance.

The two boys followed the dog out of the cave. As they emerged into the sunlight, cold water sloshed around their feet, but Frank didn't even notice. He was gazing at the dog who was sniffing the damp sand nearby. She looked up at them, then barked and wagged her tail.

'She was waiting for us,' Frank said, giving Kai a nudge with his elbow.

'It's like she's making sure we're all right,' Kai added.

'Coco!' The dog and the boys turned towards the yell. A man in running gear was racing towards them. 'Coco!'

The dog barked again and ran towards the man. He scooped her up in his arms.

Kai grinned, walking over the damp sand, away from the sea. 'That must be her owner.'

Frank nodded, following Kai. Over the man's shoulder he could see Mum and Lara and everyone else from the picnic running towards them, too.

Seconds later they were together – and all talking at once.

'Frank, what happened?' Mum asked, her face pale. 'Are you all right?'

Everyone, including Coco's owner, crowded around Frank as he explained what had happened inside the cave.

Frank blushed as he got to the end of the story. He glanced at Lara, who was still trying to catch her breath after so much sprinting. Then he looked at Kai, who had calmed Coco and who was now gazing at his feet, once again too shy to speak.

53

'Thank you so much,' said Coco's owner, setting the dog down on the sand. 'I think you may have saved Coco's life.'

'It was a team rescue,' Frank said, pointing to the others. 'We did it together.'

* * *

The rest of their trip to the beach passed in no time. Frank and Lara had to tell the story of what happened over and over again, and Frank made sure to encourage Kai to chip in every now and then, too.

Coco's owner couldn't stop thanking them. He even let them play with Coco and throw sticks for her to chase. Frank stroked Coco's back every time she came near him. How could he have ever thought she was scary?

The ice creams the grown-ups had brought back had completely melted by the time Coco's owner took her away. So before he left the beach, he bought everyone fresh ones.

Frank ate his treat sitting in the sunshine on the picnic rug – with his cousin Lara and his new friend, Kai.

Ice cream had never tasted better.